Everything You Need to Know About

BEING
ADOPTED

Adults have many reasons for adopting children. But just like biological parents, they want to have a family and a happy home.

Everything You Need to Know About

BEING ADOPTED

Laura Kaminker

THE ROSEN PUBLISHING GROUP, INC.
NEW YORK

For Liz

Published in 1999 by The Rosen Publishing Group, Inc.
29 East 21st Street, New York, NY 10010

First Edition

Library of Congress Cataloging-in-Publication Data

Kaminker, Laura.
   Everything you need to know about being adopted / Laura Kaminker.—1st ed.
            p.   cm. — (The need to know library)
   Includes bibliographical references and index.
   ISBN 0-8239-2834-9
   1. Adoption. I. Title. II. Series.
   HV875.K33 1998
   362.73'4—dc21   98-45629
                                                           CIP

Manufactured in the United States of America

Contents

Introduction

*C*heryl stared at the pink strip, hardly believing her eyes. *Maybe it's wrong,* she thought. *These home tests aren't 100 percent accurate.* But she knew there was no mistake. She had already missed two periods, and she was beginning to suspect that she could be pregnant. Cheryl sat down on the edge of the bathtub and sighed. She wanted to have a baby one day, but she never imagined she'd become a mother while still in high school. *How could this have happened? She was always so careful! She had so many plans: college, a career. And eventually a family. But not now, not yet. What am I going to do?* she wondered over and over.

Joni and Ed held hands as they walked into the lawyer's office. They were nervous, but excited. It had been five years since they first said, "Let's start a family," and still, *it was just the two of them. The years of trying, all the money they spent, all the medical procedures—always ending in disappointment—had taken a toll on their marriage. Adopting a child was a chance to start fresh, a chance to have the baby they had always wanted.*

Seven months later, Cheryl gave birth to a baby girl, whom she called Sherrill Anne. Two days after that, Cheryl signed a legal document giving up her parental rights to the baby. That same day, Joni and Ed signed a document that said they were Sherrill Anne's legal parents. Placing her baby for adoption was the most difficult thing Cheryl had ever done. She loved Sherrill Anne, and she knew she always would. But she also knew she had made the right decision, for both the baby and herself. Joni and Ed took Sherrill Anne home. A new family was born.

There are approximately 6 million adopted people in the United States. If you were adopted, your parents—the people who raised you—are not your biological parents. Your mother did not give birth to you. Because you were adopted, you naturally have questions and concerns that your non-adopted friends don't share. You may not know anyone else who was adopted. Or you may have a friend or sibling who was also adopted, but you may not talk about adoption or share your thoughts and feelings with that person.

This book explores what it means to be adopted. It

You may have questions or personal issues regarding adoption.
This is natural as you approach the teen years.

discusses the special issues that you, as an adopted person, may deal with, questions you may want to ask, and things you may wonder about. This book also discusses why many adopted people choose to search for their biological parents. The book may help you decide if you want to search for your birth parents and give you an idea of what to expect if you do search.

Although some children are born into the family that raises them, others are adopted. Adoptive families have all the love— and all the ups and downs—of biological families.

Chapter 1

What Does It Mean to Be Adopted?

Cara and Julie were waiting for their mothers to pick them up from softball practice. When Cara's mother pulled up, Julie was surprised that Cara's mother didn't look like her—Cara was Asian, but her mother was white. Julie said, "Hey, I thought you said you were Korean. How come your mom's not Korean?"

"Because I'm adopted," said Cara.

"What does that mean?" asked Julie.

Cara shrugged. "I can't explain it. I'm adopted, that's all."

There is more than one kind of family, and there is more than one way to have children. Some parents, for many different reasons, decide they would like to adopt a child. If you were adopted, your parents made the important decision to love and raise you as their own. Even though your parents did not physically conceive you and give birth to you, they are legally your parents. More important, they are your parents because they have raised you, loved you, and have always taken care of you. They are responsible for your well-being, and you have lived together as a family for all or most of your life.

Being adopted also means that you will most likely not know who your birth parents are, unless your adoptive parents know who they are or you search for them. And searching does not always mean you will find them. Knowing that you may never see your birth parents can cause a range of emotions. You may feel angry, isolated, or cheated. You may feel that no one understands who you are. You think they couldn't possibly know you because they don't know your birth parents. Or you may not care about who your birth parents are. No matter how you feel, being adopted is something that you will think about. It may be something that doesn't bother you, or it may be something that consumes your life.

There may come a time when you have to deal with difficult questions from friends or even discrimination from others. You may find it hard to answer your friends' questions or deal with insults and still feel good about yourself. Remember: There is nothing wrong with being adopted. You are just as special as someone who was not adopted. You can talk to your parents about situations like these. Together, you can come up with ways of handling them that work for you.

When people talk about adoption, they use special words and expressions. You've probably heard some of these words, but some of them may be new to you. Here is a list of words that are used throughout this book (and in most information about adoption) and their meanings.

adoptee - a person who was adopted

birth mother - a woman who gives birth to a baby and places it for adoption

adoptive parents - people who adopt a child; your parents, if you are an adoptee

adoptive family - all the members of a family that was brought together by adoption; you, your parents, and any siblings with whom you were raised

biological siblings - sisters and brothers who have the same birth mother or father; they may be raised in different families

adoption agency - an organization that matches birth mothers or children available for adoption with adoptive families

adoption triad - a birth mother, adoptive parents, and adoptee

Being adopted usually means you have a lot of questions about who you are and where you came from. Your adoptive parents can help answer some of your questions, but there are going to be some questions that won't be easy to answer. And that can be frustrating. Some adopted people find that learning about their background and heritage helps ease that frustration.

Chapter 2

Questions Adopted People Ask

All children are curious about themselves and their lives. We like knowing how our parents met, and what their lives were like before we were born. We want to know the story of our birth. We like hearing stories about ourselves when we were babies. As an adoptee, you have questions that your non-adopted friends don't. Some may include:

- Who are my birth parents?
- Why didn't my birth parents raise me?
- What do my birth parents look like?
- How old were my birth parents when they had me?
- Do my birth parents have other children? Do I have siblings somewhere I have never met?
- Do my birth parents love me?

As an adoptee, you may wonder about your roots. You should not feel guilty for having questions about your birth parents.

- If my birth mother loved me, why didn't she raise me?
- Why did my parents adopt me instead of, or in addition to, having biological children?
- What is my original culture?

These and other questions about adoption are completely natural and normal. We all wonder about ourselves. It's part of growing up. As an adoptee, a special set of circumstances brought you to your family and caused you to be the person you are. It's very natural to wonder how that happened and want to know all about it.

Still, many adoptees feel guilty about these thoughts and feelings. You may feel that thinking about your birth parents is wrong, that you are being disloyal to your parents or betraying their love. But this is not true! Wondering about your birth mother or birth parents doesn't mean you don't love your adoptive parents. It's just your natural curiosity about where you came from. Give yourself permission to think these thoughts and ask these questions.

Researching Your Heritage

One way to try to answer some questions about your past is to research your heritage. Learning more about your roots can yield wonderful information that can help you feel closer to where you come from.

Many adoptees come from a cultural or ethnic background different from that of their adoptive families. For

Researching your cultural heritage or country of origin may strengthen your sense of identity.

example, many Americans adopt children from Asian countries, such as Korea, China, or Cambodia, or from Latin American countries, such as Ecuador, Colombia, or Guatemala. These are called "transnational adoptions," because they take place across different countries. Children who are adopted this way may look very different from their parents.

Many adoptees raised in families of different ethnic backgrounds find that they would like to learn about their own heritage. It's okay to want to learn the language and customs of your original country, or to visit it one day. It doesn't mean that you have to reject your adoptive parents' heritage. You can observe as many traditions as you like. Your adoptive parents may want to help you learn more about your heritage. Doing this together can bring you and your parents closer together.

There are many ways to learn about your heritage. You can read books about your cultural background or make traditional food from your culture. There are also groups you can join where you can meet other people your age with the same ethnic background. Some adoptees have found it difficult to be accepted into cultural groups if they weren't raised in the culture. Don't get discouraged. If you give it time, you may find yourself feeling more comfortable. If you are open to the possibilities, you may find many great ways to learn more about your roots.

Chapter 3

Issues That Adopted Teenagers Face

*W*hen I turned eighteen, I started to think about my birth mother all the time. That's how old she was when she had me. I kept wondering, would I have a baby, too? Am I like her?

Until I was fifteen, my name was Josh. On my fifteenth birthday, my parents and I went to court to change my name to Juan. Juan was my original name, the name my birth mother gave me. I feel really good about being Juan. It feels right to me.

When I was growing up, I was the only Asian in my school. When I got to college, I joined the Korean-American Students Association. It was so great to meet other people who looked like me! But they all came from homes where Korean was spoken. They knew all about Korean culture. I found that I was still an outsider, even there.

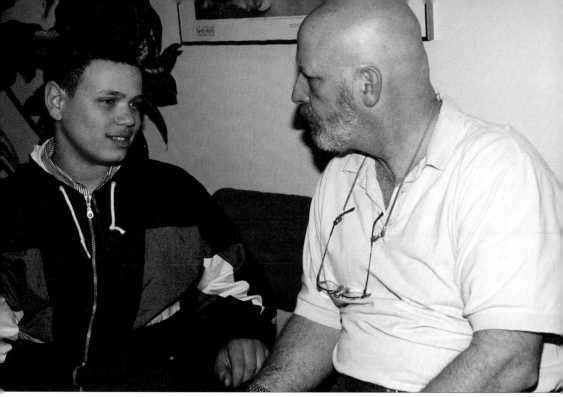

Adoptees often face complicated issues, but talking to a trusted adult may help them find answers to their questions.

When I was little, I told someone I was adopted, and he said, "What's wrong with you? Why didn't your mother keep you?" Believe me, I wasn't so quick to announce it again.

During adolescence, when girls begin to develop into women and boys start to become men, life is full of questions. As teenagers, we question many things that we took for granted as children. We also have new, very important questions about our identity and sexuality.

Adopted teenagers have the same issues, and ask the same questions, as every other teenager. But for adoptees, the questions may be a little more confusing, and the answers may be a little harder to find. During your teenage years, you may find yourself thinking about your birth parents more often, and your thoughts may start to affect your life. You may become overwhelmed with the fact that you are adopted. You may have a strong desire to connect with your birth parents in order to figure out who you are.

The Search for an Identity

During our teenage years, we are sorting out who we want to be and searching for our identities. This isn't something we're aware of; it's just part of life. But the search for identity is harder if you don't know anyone who is biologically related to you. You may wonder, What did my birth mother look like when she was my age? Do I look like her? What troubles did she have? Will I have the same problems? These questions are difficult to answer and may bother you if you don't have information about your birth mother.

Adolescence is also the time when we begin to break away from our families and establish our independence. Teenagers often feel alienated from their families—they feel that they are different and that they don't fit in. If you are an adoptee, these feelings may be stronger, simply because you were adopted. If you look different from the rest of your family, you may become more aware of those differences, and they may bother you more. Some adult adoptees say they never felt they completely fit in with their families. If this is the case for you, those feelings may become stronger when you are a teenager.

An adoptee who is of an ethnic background different from the rest of his family may become more aware of those difference as he reaches his teens.

Having a Different Ethnic Background

If you were born in a different country than your parents, or if you are of a different race or ethnic background, you may find yourself wondering more about your original race or culture. You may start to question your ethnic identity, or change how you identify yourself. For example, if you were born in Russia, and your adoptive parents are American, you may wonder if you are Russian, American, or Russian American. You may feel uncomfortable having a different ethnic background than your parents.

If you encounter prejudice or bigotry due to your race or ethnic background, it is much harder to deal with if your parents don't share the same background. You may not even tell your parents about your experiences because you don't want to upset them, or you think they won't understand. Even though your parents may not come from the same background, they have experienced many things in life, and they may know how to help you—or help you find the advice you need. If you talk with your parents, you may learn that you have a great source of support right in your own family.

Sex and Sexuality

All teenagers think about sex and their own sexuality. As an adoptee, you might wonder if your parents are good role models for you in this area. You may wonder, if my parents couldn't have babies, does that mean they don't have sex? You may imagine that your birth parents were extremely active sexually or had sex at a very young age. In reality, none of these scenarios may be true. But your own developing sexuality may lead you to wonder about it.

Low Self-Esteem

Some adoptees are very sensitive to rejection and struggle with issues of self-esteem. People with low self-esteem lack confidence and don't think very highly of themselves. Everyone wants to be liked, and no one enjoys being rejected. But while a person with strong

Many adoptees suffer from feelings of low self-esteem and rejection.

self-esteem would feel, "It's okay if he or she doesn't like me, I'm still a good person," a person with low self-esteem may feel extremely hurt. People with low self-esteem are more likely to interpret (and misinterpret) other people's actions as rejection. Some adopted people find themselves doing this often.

According to some experts, this is because, deep inside, some adoptees feel that they were rejected by their birth mothers. They feel worthless and unlovable. They may understand that their birth mothers made the decision they believed was best for them, but still feel rejected. Of course, these feelings don't apply to all adoptees, and different people feel them to different degrees.

Adoptees often encounter discrimination. Attacks like these are based on ignorance, but can be very hurtful.

Prejudice from Others

As an adoptee, you may encounter prejudice and ignorance about the fact that you were adopted. A classmate, teacher, or neighbor may have ideas about adoption based on ignorance, stereotypes, or false assumptions. That can lead to hurtful statements or teasing, which can make you feel bad about yourself.

Every Person Is Unique

It is very important to remember that not all adoptees will relate to every issue in this book, and different people will relate in different ways. One adopted person might wonder vaguely about his original culture. Another might spend all her time in the library studying about it, and save all her money for a trip to the country of her birth. One adoptee might be extremely troubled by issues of sexuality and self-esteem, while another sails through his teenage years with little problem.

Your situation is unique to you. If you find that as an adoptee you are grappling with many issues, speak to a friend or adult about your thoughts and concerns. He or she can help you sort through your feelings. Many times it helps just to be able to talk about your feelings out loud.

Chapter 4

Secret Thoughts and Feelings

We all have thoughts and feelings we don't share with anyone else. That's just part of being human. As an adoptee, you probably think about your birth parents, your adoptive family, and the fact that you were adopted. Not all your feelings are going to be positive and happy. Following are some questions that you may have asked yourself at one time.

- I get angry at my birth mother. Why didn't she keep me? Even though in my mind I know it was for the best, in my heart I still wonder, couldn't she have kept me?
- Do my parents love me less than they love my sister, who is their biological child? They say they love us both the same, but sometimes I still wonder.
- I think about my birth mother every day.

Certain issues facing adoptees can cause feelings of anger or jealousy. If you can talk to your parents about your feelings, it will probably make you feel better.

- I'm jealous of my brother because he wasn't adopted.
- I feel different from everyone in my family. I don't think I fit in.
- Are my parents disappointed because they had to adopt instead of having a baby of their own?
- I have two half-sisters—children that my birth mother kept. Why couldn't she have kept me? Sometimes I wish she had. I could never tell my parents, though. They would be so hurt.

You may be angry at your birth mother, jealous of non-adopted siblings, or resentful of your biological siblings who grew up with your birth mother. You may be angry at your adoptive parents; you may wonder why

29

they adopted you. You may wish you hadn't been adopted, or wish you had been adopted by different parents. Most adopted people have thoughts and feelings like these at various times in their lives, especially when they are teenagers. Some people will be very troubled by these thoughts and feelings; others will think about them only briefly.

All your thoughts and feelings about being adopted are natural and normal. But many adoptees feel guilty about their private thoughts. Perhaps you know that your parents tried hard to have a family, and that they suffered while they were trying. You don't want their lives to be more difficult. Perhaps you've been told that you are very lucky to be adopted, and that your life is so much better than it would have been with your birth mother. You don't want to seem ungrateful. Knowing how much your adoptive parents love you, you don't want to be disloyal to them by thinking about your birth parents. And you love your adoptive parents and don't want to hurt them.

There is no need to feel guilty about your thoughts and feelings. Being an adopted child is complicated. Though it is mostly a positive experience, it is not without its sadness and difficulties. And so your feelings about being adopted are also complex and contradictory. You love your parents and resent them, you miss your birth mother and are angry at her—both at the same time. These are natural human emotions and are nothing to feel guilty about. Remember, your thoughts can't hurt anyone. You are allowed to feel whatever you feel.

In a support group, you may discover that others share your questions and concerns. In a group, you can learn ways to cope with your problems.

If you have a friend or a sibling who is also adopted, try talking about some of your feelings with him or her. Many adoptees find it very beneficial to join an adoptee support group. In the group, they hear other adoptees talk about their feelings about adoption, and they share their own feelings. Through a group, you can see that your feelings are truly natural and normal, and that most adoptees share them. Here are comments from adoptees whose lives have been enriched by support groups.

I used to feel so alone with my thoughts. Since I started going to the meetings, I don't feel so lonely anymore.

31

When I first came to the group, I was amazed. Here were people expressing feelings I had felt all my life but had never spoken out loud.

Support groups provide an opportunity for people to meet others who are experiencing similar situations in life. Knowing that you are not alone and that there are people who are going through the same things in life can be a great relief. Support groups also allow members to learn from one another's experiences. If you are interested in meeting people who are dealing with the same things you are, give a support group a try.

Chapter 5

Your Birth Records

As an adoptee, you have two birth certificates: the original, which gives the names of your birth parents, and a second one with the names of your adoptive parents. As an American adoptee, unless you were born in a state with open records, you are not legally allowed to see your original birth certificate.

In most countries, when an adoptee reaches the age of legal adulthood—eighteen or twenty-one, depending on where the person lives—he or she can request and receive a copy of his or her original birth certificate. But in order to see his or her original birth certificate, an adoptee in the United States must go through a formal court proceeding. The exceptions are adoptees born in Kansas, Hawaii, or Alaska. They can see their records when they are eighteen without going to court.

If you decide to search for your biological parents, you will have to look through several records. Unfortunately, some of them may be closed.

The laws that forbid adoptees from seeing their birth records dictate that those records remain "closed," or inaccessible to the adoptee. Laws about closed records date back to a time when attitudes about sex, family, and adoption were very different. In the past, it was considered shameful for an unmarried woman to have a child. Keeping birth records a secret was supposed to keep people from knowing that a woman had had a baby before she was married. This was intended to protect the woman from social shame. Closed records were also intended to protect a child whose parents were not married from the same shame.

Also, many couples who were infertile (could not conceive biological children) didn't want other people to know they couldn't have children of their own. So keeping birth records a secret was intended to protect everyone involved in the adoption.

Opposition to Closed Records

Now that society's attitudes have changed, many people feel the laws should be brought up to date. Most adoptees feel that the closed-records laws are discriminatory (they unfairly single out a group of people for unequal treatment under the law) since all non-adopted Americans have access to their own birth records.

Many people also feel that closed records make life harder for adoptees. First, closed records hide answers to adoptees' important questions. In addition, closed records imply that there is something wrong or shameful about adoption. Most psychologists and social workers who work in the adoption field, along with many adoptive parents, believe that adoptees should have access to their original birth certificates.

Support for Closed Records

In the United States, adoption birth records are predominantly closed. Forty-seven states have closed records. People who think the laws should not be changed say that a birth mother must have the right to remain anonymous (unknown) if she prefers. Yet even in countries with open records, such as England and Australia, a birth mother may choose to remain anonymous. Very few birth mothers choose this option.

Supporters of closed records also believe that if birth records are opened, women who are pregnant but cannot keep the baby will be more likely to choose abortion. They believe that opening birth records will cause the abortion rate to rise. However, there is no evidence to support this. States and countries with open birth records do not have higher abortion rates than those with closed records.

What Is an Open Adoption?

Since the 1930s, when courts and adoption agencies got involved in adoption, adoptive parents have not known who their child's birth parents were. And it was assumed that an adoptee would never know his or her

Talk to your adoptive parents before you try to locate your biological family. It is good to have their support and understanding as you pursue this goal.

birth parents. In one kind of open adoption, the adoptive parents and the birth parents exchange information and often meet. An increasing number of adoptions are being conducted this way.

Still, advocates for open records say this is not really an open adoption, because only the adoptive *parents* have legal access to the information. If the parents decide not to share the information with their child, the adoptee has no legal right to access it. If the adoptive parents die, the adoptee has no right to see his or her birth records.

In a true open adoption, adoptive parents tell the adoptee who his or her birth parents are. If you are from an open-adoption family, you probably have seen pictures of your birth parents. You may have a letter or gift from your birth mother or birth parents. One day, you will be given the opportunity to meet and, if you choose, have a relationship with her or them. Or your birth mother or parents may have been involved in your life all along, as part of your extended family.

Many people believe open adoptions are healthier than traditional adoptions. Adoptees from open adoptions are given honest information about themselves, so that they can have a more complete picture of themselves and feel more secure. But it's important to remember that every adoption is unique. Adoptions take place under widely different circumstances and for many different reasons. Open adoptions are not always possible and would not always be beneficial to the adoptee.

Even though more adoptive parents are choosing open adoption, the legal rights of adoptees have not changed. Adoptees who do not grow up in an open-adoption family still do not have the legal right to information about the beginning of their own lives.

Chapter 6

Why Search?

T housands of adoptees are searching for their biological relatives. The number of adoptees who decide to search is increasing every year. Searching does not mean they are unhappy with their adoptive families. These adoptees are not looking for new families. They feel they have much to gain by finding their biological family, or at least by learning about them.

There are many reasons for searching. Some people search for medical reasons. They want to know their birth family's medical history to be aware of any hereditary diseases. Many adoptees feel a great yearning to know who their parents are. They feel that something central to their lives is missing—something the rest of the world takes for granted—and they want to fill in that missing piece. Some adoptees feel it is very important to connect with their original ethnic heritage. And many therapists have found that when adoptees are troubled by certain issues, searching helps bring them greater inner peace.

When I was in junior high and high school, I had a lot of trouble with guys. I found myself gravitating toward unhealthy relationships, and I took the breakups really, really hard. I was definitely developing some dangerous patterns. My therapist said, "Maybe it's time to ask your parents about your birth mother." Now that I write to my birth mother, my life has calmed down a lot. I'm much more together.

Many non-adopted people don't understand why adoptees want to search for their birth families. Some people ask, If you already have parents who love you, why do you want to find the people who gave you away? How could finding your biological mother help you find out who you are?

You might find these questions difficult to answer. It might be hard for you to explain why you want to search, because to you, it seems like the most natural thing in the world. In this respect, the life experience of a person who was adopted is very different from that of a person who was not.

Not every adoptee wants to search for his or her birth parents. And searching means different things to different people. Searching may mean writing a letter, seeing a picture, getting the answers to certain questions.

Some people might not understand why you want to search for your birth parents. If this is your choice, you should pursue it, but only when you feel you are ready.

It doesn't necessarily mean having an ongoing relationship with your birth parents, or even meeting them.

I've spoken to lots of adoptees in their early adolescence who find their birth parents. They start writing to them, and the birth parents are all excited about meeting them, and the adoptive parents are excited about it too. But the child says, "No, thanks, I just wanted this letter and this picture." What's right for one person isn't right for another. People need help and support while they figure out what's right for them.

Along with the positive reasons to search for your birth parents, there are some reasons that are not so healthy. Like a lot of teenagers—adopted and non-adopted—you may be having trouble getting along with your parents. If you are adopted, however, you may have a fantasy that if you lived with your birth parents, you wouldn't have these problems. Part of your desire to find your birth parents could be your anger at your parents and your desire to get away from them.

Deciding whether or not to search for your birth parents is a serious step. Your decision shouldn't be based on anger, or on a fantasy about escaping. Remember, you aren't finding new parents. Even if you find your birth parents, you will still live with your adoptive parents.

Your decision to locate your birth parents can change the lives of your entire family. It is important that your reasons for this search have been carefully thought out.

Chapter 7

What If I Do Search?

If you think you want to learn more about your birth parents, and possibly write to them or meet them one day, one of the first things to do is to talk to your adoptive parents.

The decision to search is a big step, and it can be a scary one. The search itself can be a long and painful process. And the answers to your questions may be painful too. No adoptee of any age should go through it alone. But if you are a teenager still living at home, trying to conduct a search on your own is an especially bad idea.

On a purely practical level, if you are under eighteen, you will need your parents' permission to see your adoption records. Your parents may also have information about your birth parents that would be useful to your search.

But beyond that, if you don't tell your parents that you are thinking about searching, you are keeping an important part of yourself hidden from them. This can make you feel isolated and misunderstood. If you feel guilty about wanting to find your birth parents, keeping your desire a secret will only increase your feelings of guilt. But telling your parents can be scary, since you do not know how they will react.

I was terrified of how my parents would react. Would they be hurt? Would they think this meant I wished they weren't my parents? Would they try to prevent me from searching? I even wondered, Would they still love me?

I was so scared to tell my mother that I wanted to search. I was sure she'd burst out in tears, or have a heart attack or something. But she just looked at me and said, "I was wondering when you were going to ask." Then she left the room and came back with a shoe box. She had all the information. She was just waiting for me to ask.

When adoptees tell their parents that they want to search, they are often very surprised at their parents' reaction. The reaction is usually much more positive than they expect. Your adoptive parents will probably not be surprised that you have questions about your origins. They may have had counseling before the adoption to help them prepare, and they may have read about the issues that are involved.

Your family might feel a little threatened at first if you search for your birth parents, but chances are good that they will understand your reasons.

When I was sixteen, my mother asked me if I wanted to meet my birth mother. I wasn't sure how I felt about it at first. Mostly it was very scary, and I had to think about it for a while. Then when I decided, yes, I wanted to meet her, my mother freaked out! We all thought it was kind of strange, since the whole reunion thing was her idea. But she was scared she was going to lose me. We had a few sessions of family therapy, so everyone could feel more comfortable and get ready for the change. My mom needed to be reassured that I still loved her, that I wasn't trying to replace her.

When you tell your parents that you are thinking of searching for your birth parents, they are almost certainly going to be scared. It's a big change in their lives, and change is always scary. They love you very much, and they don't know what will happen if you also have a relationship with your birth parents. Those feelings are natural and will probably soon pass. This is another reason to talk to your parents about searching: it will give all of you time to adjust before the actual search begins.

Search-Support Groups

Most adoptees also find it very helpful to join a support group, often called a search-support group. In the group, you will meet other adoptees of all ages. Some will be in the process of searching; some will have completed their searches; others will be deciding whether or not to search. You will be able to get practical advice about searching, but, more important, you will be able to discuss your feelings with people who are in the exact same situation as you. If you are thinking about searching but are afraid to tell your parents, the search-support group can help you with that too. To find a search-support group in your area, try calling one of the organizations listed in the back of this book.

Is It Possible to Find My Birth Parents?

Despite closed records, most adoptees who search are able to find their birth parents. Some searches take several years and are very expensive. Other searches take only a few months and don't cost very much money.

At times, your search for your birth parents may be stressful. There are several hotlines and support groups you can call to find help with the problems you encounter.

Most adoptees who search do find their birth mothers or find truthful information about them. The vast majority of birth mothers who are contacted by children they placed for adoption do want to meet and speak to them. There are, however, adoptees who cannot find their birth parents. And there are a few birth mothers who do not want to be contacted.

No matter what the outcome, most adoptees who have searched are very glad they did. They may not have found what they were dreaming of, but the search makes them feel more secure and more complete.

If I Find My Birth Mother, What Place Will She Have in My Life?

This is the enormous question facing every adoptee who decides to search. It is a question that no one can answer for you.

Reunions with birth parents are scary. They can be joyous, and they can be painful. They are usually both. Once you have information about your birth parents and your questions are answered, it is up to you to decide where to go from there. You don't have to decide anything right away. And you can make different decisions at different times, as your life changes and your feelings change. What's right for you at sixteen may not be right when you are twenty or twenty-five. In this part of your life, no one can make you do anything you are not ready for or comfortable with. You are in charge.

When I was nineteen, my mother said to me, "The agency called. Your birth mother wrote you a letter; she wants to meet you." It came as a complete shock. I received one letter, and I wrote one letter. We sent each other pictures, and I got to ask her all the questions I've always wondered about. That was thrilling! But I didn't want to go further. Then we wrote each other letters, but always through the agency. I didn't give her my address. After a while, I gave my birth mother my address, so she could write to me directly. But I still haven't met her. I think I will one day. But I'm not ready yet.

More Than Just Parents

A search for your biological family often yields more than birth parents. There may be siblings, possibly grandparents, aunts, uncles, and cousins. For some adoptees, this is the best—and hardest—part of the reunion.

When I searched, my birth mother had already died. It was very painful to accept that I would never meet her. But I did find a brother and several cousins. That's been very wonderful and comforting to me.

I am getting to know my birth mother. I'm also getting to know her two sons—my new brothers—and my grandfather. My adoptive parents' parents died when I was very young or before I was born, so I never had grandparents before. This was a totally unexpected benefit of searching.

When you are reunited with your biological family, you may find not only parents, but also brothers, sisters, nieces, nephews, and cousins!

As soon as I met my biological sister, we were best friends. We have so much in common! I feel closer to her than anyone else on earth. But sometimes I get so angry! It's so unfair that we didn't meet until we were twenty, that we didn't grow up together. I know why my birth mother did what she did, but it still makes me sad and angry. I wish I had known my sister earlier. But I'm really glad we have each other now.

Every year, thousands of babies are adopted and are raised in happy, loving homes.

Chapter 8

Conclusion

Every year, thousands of families adopt babies and children. There are three sides to every adoption: the birth mother or parents, the adoptive parent or parents, and the adoptee. Although adoption is mostly a joyous and positive event, it also has a somber or sad side, because a mother and father were not able to raise their baby.

In most ways, adopted people are just like non-adopted people. But, as you've learned, adoptees have certain questions and concerns that non-adopted people don't. As an adoptee, you probably wonder about your birth parents. Like other adoptees, you wonder, Did my birth mother love me? Why wasn't she able to raise me? You wonder what your birth parents looked like. These questions, and many others like them, are completely natural and normal. All adoptees think about them, and

It is natural for adoptees to wonder about their birth parents and background, but most find the love and guidance they need from their adoptive families.

many find that when they become teenagers, they think about them more often.

Some adopted people find that they are troubled by low self-esteem, oversensitivity to rejection, and questions about their identity. Though non-adopted teenagers—and people of every age—also struggle with these issues, some experts believe that being an adopted child increases your chances of struggling with these problems.

Many adoptees find that searching for their birth parents, or just getting truthful information about them, helps them resolve some concerns. Whether or not you are disturbed by these issues, knowing more about your origins may bring you greater happiness and inner peace.

At this time, most adoptees in the United States are not legally allowed to see their original birth records. However, most adoptees who search for their birth parents are able to find them. If you are considering searching for your birth parents or researching your roots, there's no need to do it on your own. Thousands of adoptees have been through the same experience. They can offer help and advice through support groups.

All experts, including adoptees who have searched, strongly recommend that you speak to your parents about your desire to search. Your desire to connect with your birth family is not wrong in any way. Your parents might have information that could help your search and they might want to help you. You'll feel better about yourself and your decision if you are open with them.

Most adoptees find it difficult to tell their parents that they are interested in searching, but then are surprised by their parents' positive reactions.

Not all adoptees want to search for their birth parents, and no one should search until and unless he or she is ready. The important thing to remember is that it's your choice. Take the time to ask yourself what you want to do. Write down your thoughts or talk to someone about how you feel. Ask yourself how you feel about being adopted. You may find that you are feeling strong emotions that you have been ignoring.

Give yourself time to think about your feelings. Then you can think about making an honest decision with yourself about your future.

Glossary

adoption The process through which an infant or child is placed in a home with people other than the birth parents. These people are given parental rights over the child. They are responsible for his or her welfare.

closed records Birth records that are forbidden by law for adoptees to see.

hereditary disease A disease passed from a parent to his or her child.

heritage The traditions and customs of a person's original culture.

identity The qualities or traits that make up a person's personality.

open adoption Adoption agreement between adoptive parents and the birth parents that allows contact when the adopted person grows up.

open records Birth records that are available by
law for adoptees to see.

prejudice An adverse judgment or opinion formed
beforehand or without knowledge of the facts.

search-support group A group of adoptees who
are in the process of searching for, have completed
their search, or are deciding whether or not to
search for their biological parents.

self-esteem One's feeling about oneself.

transnational adoption Adoptions that take place
across different countries.

Where to Go for Help

American Adoption Congress
1000 Connecticut Avenue NW
Washington, DC 20036
(202) 483-3399

Center for Family Connections
350 Cambridge Street
Cambridge, MA 02139
(617) 547-0909

National Adoption Information Clearinghouse (naic)
P.O. Box 1182
Washington, DC 20013
Web site: http://ww.calib.com/naic

Hotlines

Concerned United Birth Parents
(800) 822-2777

Council for Equal Rights in Adoption
(212) 988-0110

In Canada

Adoption Resource Center
3216 Yonge Street, 2nd Floor
Toronto, ON M4N 2L2
(416) 482-0021

Web Sites

BirthQuest
http://www.access.digex.net/

Adoptee Searcher's Handbook
http://www.login.net/inverc/search.htm

For Further Reading

Cohen, Shari. *Coping with Being Adopted.* New York:
Rosen Publishing Group, 1988.

Gabel, Susan. *Filling in the Blanks: A Guided Look at
Growing Up Adopted.* Indianapolis, IN: Perspectives
Press, 1988.

Gravelle, Karen, and Susan Fischer. *Where Are My Birth
Parents? A Guide for Teenage Adoptees.* New York:
Walker and Co., 1995.

Krementz, Jill. *How It Feels to Be Adopted.* New York:
Alfred A. Knopf, 1988.

Messner, Julian. *Adoption: The Facts, Feelings, and Issues
of a Double Heritage.* Parsippany, NJ: Silver Burdett
Press, 1990.

Pohl, Constance, and Kathleen K. Harns. *Transracial
Adoption: Children and Parents Speak.* New York:
Franklin Watts, 1992.

Strauss, Jean A. *Birthright: The Guide to Search and
Reunion for Adoptees.* New York: Viking Penguin,
1994.

Index

Acknowledgments
The author thanks everyone who shared their thoughts and feelings about adoption with her. Very special thanks to Dr. Joyce Pavao for her time and expertise.

About the Author
Laura Kaminker has been a freelance writer for thirteen years. She has written books, magazine articles, and educational videos, and has worked with teenagers as a teacher and counselor. Laura's article about girls who were adopted appeared in *Seventeen* magazine. She lives in New York City with her partner, Allan Wood, and their two dogs.

Photo Credits
Cover by TK, pp. 8, 10, 16, 18, 21, 23, 25, 29, 34, 47, 52, 54 by Ira Fox; pp. 2, 49 by Lauren Piperno; p. 26 by Ethan Zindler; p. 31 by Guillemina de Ferrari; p. 37 by Seth Dinnerman; pp. 42, 44, 56 by Les Mills.